I'm Free: A Memoir for Grief and Pain

LaVetra Sullivan

© 2023 LaVetra Sullivan
I'm Free: A Memoir for Grief and Pain
Kingdom Builders Publications, LLC

All rights reserved. No part of this book may be reproduced or transmitted in any form or by any means without written permission from the author.
Scriptures marked ESV are taken from The Holy Bible, English Standard Version®.
Scriptures marked KJV are taken from the King James Version.
Scriptures marked NIV are taken from The Holy Bible, New International Version®.
Scriptures marked NKJV are taken from the New King James Version®.
Scriptures marked NLT are taken from The Holy Bible, New Living Translation®.
Scriptures marked NRS are taken from the New Revised Standard Version Bible.

ISBN
978-1-0880-9844-8

LCCN
2023905368

Author
LaVetra Sullivan

Contributing Writers
Alice Baker
Adella Elmore
Kamilah Legette
Diamond Sullivan

Editor
Lakisha S. Forrester

Cover Design
Original inspirational design
Diamond Sullivan
LoMar Designs
Printed in U.S.A.

Acknowledgements

Jackie Elmore, Sr. and Adella Elmore, Jackie Elmore, Jr., William Elmore, John and Vernell Elmore, James and Diane Elmore, Myra Elmore, Gerard Elmore, Mamie Anderson Kershaw, Emerald Sullivan, Diamond Sullivan, George and Octavia Wilmore, Milton Wilmore, Nauria Wilmore, Barbara Calhoun, Prophetess Alice Baker, Kamilah Legette, Alexis and Acaci Brooks, Joe and Cynthia Seawright, Shana, Shayla, and Aliyah Seawright, friends, and family.

Preface

The death of a loved one is a hard pill to swallow. Sometimes it eats at our souls because we have shared so many memories with that person. It hurts to see your loved one leave this earth, especially if you feel it is before the person's time. However, we never know when a person will leave us. It is my hope that this short memoir will help you through the grieving process. We will never forget our loved ones, but with time, the pain will ease knowing he or she is with God.

After my brother passed, I can remember my aunt asking my mother how she got over it. My mom replied, "Honey, you never get over it; you get through it." Those words stuck with me. When I watched my niece transition, I knew the days ahead would be long and hard, but I remembered my mother's words. I knew that at some point, the dark clouds would lift, and the Lord would give our family beauty for ashes.

This book is written to encourage you that you will get through the hurt and pain from the passing of your loved one. You may think that your wounds will never heal, but with time, God will heal all pain. You must focus on God each and every day of your life. I pray that He will lift the heaviness from your life. Grieving is a process, which means it will come to an end. You will begin to smile and remember the joyous times you had with your loved one.

It is my prayer that God touches each person who reads this book in a special way and heal his or her heart.

May He bring peace and closure to you so that you will continue to receive the blessings He has for your life.

"For I know the plans I have for you," declares the Lord, plans to prosper you and not to harm you, plans to give you hope and a future"
Jeremiah 29:11 (NIV).

To Jasmine, My Beloved Goddaughter

In Memory of You

When I think of you, a butterfly comes into my vision. Imprinted on the feathers are big colorful words. Each word represents the Fruit of the Spirit. As you unfolded, you became the words on that butterfly. We did not know what you would become as you were becoming. Through your growth process and the many stages, like the butterfly, in the end, you blossomed into a beautiful and loving young lady. You represented inner and outer beauty. You made an impact on my life, your god sister's, and many others with your heart and spirit.

In reminiscing about the good times, I still hear all the words of encouragement and inspiration given. You gave so much of yourself while you were here with us. You possessed and showed so much love and so much help to others. Your compassion and kindness are deeply missed. You are resting in a more beautiful place now. Your love will always live in our minds and hearts forever. Thank you for giving my daughter, others, and me the opportunity to know you and share your love. We love you, Jasmine!

Always,

Alice Baker and Kamilah Legette

Foreword

The wing of the hospital read: "NSICU: Neuroscience Intensive Care Unit." I walked through the big doors that flung open as if they were welcoming me. I told myself to hold it together as I entered the eighth floor of the hospital. I made it in. I paused in place and stood there looking in disbelief at my cousin Jasmine. Her hair was shaved, tubes ran from the hole in her head to the machines, her frozen eyes were propped open, and her body was covered in a long white sheet. She laid there lifeless. I could not hold back my tears. I sobbed waterfalls over my mom's shoulder, drenching her shirt with my pain and grief. I called to Jasmine, but she did not get up. She did not move. She did nothing to respond. I felt the stench of death enter the room. It passed over our heads as if it held all of us to its name. Blood dripped from her brain into a bag clinging to a piece of equipment. She was only twenty years old. No husband, no children, and no college degree in Music Education.

The nurse entered the room to check her vitals. All of her organs were stable: her lungs, heart, kidneys, and liver. All of them, except her brain. As the nurse shifted us to the family meeting room, nothing made sense to me. *Why her? Why now?* I thought to myself. The doctor began to explain her condition to us.

"Her brain holds several blood clots. There is no room for pressure on her brain at this age. Her arteries will not allow blood to pass through the rest of her body. We have done everything we can. We don't know what else to do. I've never seen anything like this," he stated.

What do you mean by you don't know what to do? We sat in the waiting room for twelve hours that day to hear an experienced, educated doctor tell us that he did not have any more resources for our loved one.

"It is not looking good for her. I will have to perform an apnea test to determine if she is brain dead. If she is, legally, we will have to declare her dead," he proceeded.

Jasmine? Dead? This can't be real! This isn't real! At that moment, the memories of my dear cousin flashed before my eyes.

* * *

My mom and her sisters were all pregnant in the same year. Jasmine was born in January, I was born in May, and my cousin Nauria was born in October of 1998. Jasmine and I were extremely close. When I was younger, my family lived in Hopkins, South Carolina. Jasmine would sometimes come to our house to spend the night. Even though we were first cousins, we were more like sisters. We played dress-up and dinner with our Barbie dolls. We were interested in the Bratz dolls and tried to do our hair and makeup just like them. Sometimes I would stay at Jasmine's house. Her house was bigger than ours and we would cook together with my uncle's supervision.

When my parents divorced, we moved in with my mom's sister and her family. Even though our living situation was due to unforeseen circumstances, Jasmine and I made the best of everything. She shared her bedroom with me. We would go to sleep and snuggle really close to stay warm.

Jasmine had a love for doing hair and often talked about getting her cosmetology license. She began to braid my hair and became my hairstylist. She would also paint my fingernails and toenails with blue nail polish. Blue was her favorite color. We were so tightly knitted that I was mistakenly called Jasmine, and she was sometimes called Diamond.

Jasmine had a passion for music. Her favorite group of all time was the legendary TLC, with singers T-Boz, Left Eye, and Chilli. She adopted the name Chilli as her nickname during her teen years. She owned almost every album by the group, along with their posters and fan-based accessories. Jasmine also took a love to older music from previous generations. She would walk and sing around the house with her beautiful, angelic voice.

As we grew older, Jasmine and I became closer to each other. At the age of eighteen, we both decided to attend college. We talked about how we were going to be teachers together and help each other organize our classrooms. Jasmine decided to attend Winthrop University in Rock Hill, SC, and I decided to attend the University of South Carolina Beaufort in Bluffton, SC. We were north and south of the state, but we always kept in touch with each other. We had FaceTime, Facebook, Skype, and all other forms of social media that any amount of distance did not keep us apart.

* * *

I visited my mom the Monday after my college was out for the May 2018 semester. Jasmine was home from Winthrop, and I was ready to spend quality time with her. I had not seen her since the previous Christmas because of our schedule differences. When I visited my family for Christmas break, we discovered that Jasmine's fingers would turn purple. We knew this was unusual. The doctors thought she may have had Raynaud's disease, a condition in which the body suffers from low levels of oxygen due to limited blood circulation. Sadly, doctors did not tell us the future effects of the syndrome, especially the consequence of death. They instructed her to take Aspirin for her pain, but never gave her the information to defeat the condition, physically or mentally.

Jasmine and I did not get a chance to meet up over our spring breaks. I was in the bed when I got the call about Jasmine.

"She had a seizure. We are on the way to the emergency room," my mom communicated.

Jasmine never had a seizure before. I did not know what was going on. I did not get any rest because I was worried and deeply troubled. My mom came around in the guestroom to tell us that Jasmine did not have a seizure. It was a stroke. I automatically started looking up causes of strokes. The internet informed me that anyone can have a stroke, but it is more common among the elderly. It also explained that blood clots on the brain are the primary factors leading to strokes and could also be effects of head trauma or the bursting of a blood vessel.

I could not believe that this was happening to Jasmine. She was the trophy picture of great health and happiness. We prayed and prayed that Jasmine would make it through this traumatic experience. We had faith in God that she would rise up and walk away from this experience with a testimony in hand. Jasmine never got up. On Wednesday, May 9, 2018, at 5:23 p.m., Jasmine's spirit entered the gates of Heaven.

* * *

That night, I could not sleep. I felt like I had been run over by a dump truck. My body was numb and aching. I had lost a piece of me. My first cousin, my sister, my ride-or-die partner, and my best friend left me on the earth alone. Every time I tried to add everything up, I could not get an answer for closure. The news hurt and devastated me greatly. We did not immediately tell anyone of her death, but somehow it didn't take long for others to find out. Our Facebook pages began to flood with apologies and sincere, sympathetic messages. She was not even gone for two hours. The calls and social media posts became too much to bear. *I am still trying to wrap my mind around this. This does not even seem real.*

As the week passed, the days got harder and harder to live through. The first day, my mom and I rode to my aunt's home. I nearly had a panic attack. I never imagined being there without Jasmine unless she was away at Winthrop. We went to my aunt's house every day that week. As we cleaned up for the guests, my aunt asked me to move Jasmine's belongings to her bedroom. I had not brought myself to terms with the whole death thing yet, so I could not gain strength to open Jasmine's room door and place her possessions in there. It was all just too hard. I thought that looking at our pictures would help ease my sorrows. They only made them worse as I thought about how I would never be able to take a picture with her again.

* * *

No one is exempt from death. We believe that it is typical for our older generations to pass along first.

However, recently, it has been our younger generations taking their place. My grandmother was 79 years old at the time. She suffered from Alzheimer's disease. If there was a chance of death in our family, we were naive to think that we would lose her first. Instead, she lived to bury her young granddaughter. *We were definitely blindsided with this one, God.* At least we can say that we have a guardian angel looking over us now.

As I ride to work each morning, I still pick up the phone to call or text Jasmine, only to remember that I can't anymore. I still remember her as innocent and pure to the heart. She was just like a Jasmine flower. Her aroma stayed throughout the earth and gathered hundreds of her friends at her wake, candlelight vigil, and funeral service.

Jasmine's spirit still rests with mine. Each morning, I can hear her telling me that it's going to be alright and that she is relieved and no longer suffering in her pain. When other people die, we normally say, "I'm so sorry for your loss." However, you will never understand the true meaning of those words until death really hits home or comes knocking boldly at your front door.

Jasmine did not get a chance to finish college. She was just encountering her prime years of life. The years that we were supposed to spend continuing to grow together will never be experienced. At this moment, I can only dedicate all of my successes and future endeavors to her. The road from here on out will be tough and rocky. For me, the hurt and pain will never cease, but can be eased with the help and support of my family. The only lesson that I can say that I truly learned from this incident is to love all, just as Jasmine did; to live each day without worry and regret, just as she did; and to always be happy, just as she was.

My life changed May 9, 2018. I remind my husband, daughter, mom, and sister every day how much I love them and how much they mean to me. I am quick to forgive and slow to anger. I can say that my faith with my God has been shaken, but I will never stop believing in Him, for He is a God who makes no mistakes.

I truly miss Jasmine, but one day I will see her again. This time, her hair will flow long and freely, her eyes will glisten with beauty, and she will be clothed in a long white robe. She will sing with me again, walk and talk with me, and embrace me as I stand in her presence.

Diamond Sullivan

Reflection

Jasmine is a climbing plant that bears fragrance. Much like this beautiful flower, Jasmine has left a sweet aroma throughout Orangeburg, York, and Calhoun Counties. She was known and loved by all. She lived each day as if it was her last. She was not only my niece, but she was a daughter and a friend. Her mom always told her she acted just like me. She was my mini-me, my buddy, my friend, my right-hand man, and my family's hairstylist. Jasmine had a love for braiding hair, and I didn't mind being her guinea pig. She was a perfectionist. If it didn't look right, she was going to start over. If you said anything, she gave you the side-eye and said, "Look here, lady."

Jasmine's gift for designing was not just with hair. Each year when it was time for me to return to school, she would ask, "Lady" or "Uhh, ma'am, when do you go back to school? I'm coming to help you set up your class." Not only did she help me in my classroom, but she helped other teachers in their classes as well.

I was so excited about Jasmine's choice to attend Winthrop University and major in Music Education. I had the opportunity to attend one of her concerts as the choir toured the state. She loved music and the arts. She was a singer, a praise dancer, and a stepper.

The Saturday before she passed, we spent the day together. We were riding in the car, and I said, "So, did you have a good year?"

"Yes."

"Great. So, didn't you sing in front of the jury or judges this week?"

"Unh-huh."

Anyone who knew Jasmine knew she didn't like being asked a bunch of questions.

"How did that go?" I asked anyway.

"Good," she said.

At that time, I had no idea that four days later she would be singing in front of the Grand Juror, auditioning for the

Heavenly Choir. The Sunday before Jasmine passed, the family spent the day together. She was so excited that she was going to take the Praxis test that Tuesday to enter the education program. Around noon that day, I realized I forgot to call or text her to wish her the best on her test. Sadly, she never made it to that test.

On Wednesday, May 9, 2018, at 5:23 p.m., Jasmine passed the ultimate test and made it into the highest degree program there is. Her instructor said, *"Well done, thou good and faithful servant!"* (**Matthew 25:21**, KJV).

Jasmine always told us to never say, "Bye," but say, "See you later."

So sleep on, sweet Jasmine, take your rest. We will see you later. We all love you, but God loves you best.

Aunt Veatie

Introduction

You often hear people say, "People die every day," or "Death is a part of life." We say these phrases so loosely. I have lost close relatives in my life, which include my father and my brother, but no death has ever hit me like that of my niece. Nothing hits you harder than an unexpected curveball. It catches you off guard and you don't have time to prepare.

I don't know who this book is for, but I believe it will help someone who may be struggling with the death of a loved one. I am not a psychologist, nor am I certified to counsel anyone, but it is because of God and His Holy Spirit that I can share my experiences with you to help comfort you.

Death is never easy to accept, but it is more comforting to know that your friends and family are there to support you. After Jasmine's passing, I thanked those who came to support our family. One friend of mine said, "I didn't do anything but pray for your family."

I said, "You don't know what a difference it makes knowing you have your friends and family members to support you."

This was the first funeral I went to that I felt love from all those who attended. Everyone was grieved and shared in our pain. The services were the culmination of a week full of hurt and sorrow. Jasmine was gone and there was nothing anyone could do to bring her back.

There were numerous cards, flowers, and donations given to the family to show love and support. Our church family was there, as well as our coworkers and friends. The choir that Jasmine was on at Winthrop University rode one of the school's buses to be a part of her Homegoing Service. They gave my sister a book with journal writings from Jasmine's professors and friends expressing their love and thoughts.

Jasmine will always be remembered for the way she touched the lives of people everywhere.

In Spite of Our Circumstances, God is Sovereign and Majestic!

The days after your loved one passes are the worst days ever. Returning home and leaving them behind is an awful feeling. I never imagined having to leave my twenty-year-old niece behind in a hospital, never to see her again. Driving off that night was the worst feeling I have ever felt in my life. *How could we leave her behind? Our family never leaves anyone behind. We always include everybody in our events and functions, such as family vacations, birthday celebrations, family reunions, holidays, etc.* I did not sleep much that night. Things would never be the same.

The next day, I went to my sister's house. We had to be there for each other because a piece of us was missing. Our hearts were broken. It is hard trying to close the gap when there is a missing link in our family circle. In fact, if you think about a doughnut, there is no way that can happen. God is the only Person who can mend that broken piece.

When you lose a loved one, sometimes you may feel as if your world has ended. There may be a feeling of emptiness that you cannot describe. Only those who have experienced this pain will be able to understand what it is that you feel inside. When the world seems to cave in on you and you may have trouble remembering what day it is, it is during these times that you must focus on God who provides strength and healing. God is the only person that can help us get through these difficult times. Bad thoughts may pop into your head as you wonder how your loved one feels. Stress begins to weigh down on you and you may find yourself becoming physically sick. You must find the strength and the willpower to keep moving. You must ask yourself if your loved one would want you to stop living. Pain is real and it hurts so much when our loved one has left this world, but we cannot stay in this place forever. In the midst of our pain, we must know that God sees and knows it all. Knowing God is sovereign means knowing He is in control of everything. We must rely on Him to heal us from all hurt and pain.

"He heals the brokenhearted and bandages their wounds"
Psalm 147:3 (NLT).

God does not always give us answers; He gives us the power to overcome.

We prayed for Jasmine's immediate healing. We wanted to see her walk again. We prayed that God would restore her health; that she would rise up and do the things she liked to do. She was way too young. At the age of twenty, Jasmine was fighting for her life. Who would have ever thought she would die so young? There were no warning signs. No time to prepare. Within twenty-four hours, she was gone. Gone! Gone! Way too soon!

Why didn't God perform a miracle like He did for Lazarus? He had done it before. Why didn't He do it again? She was such a beautiful girl. She was so well-mannered and full of life. We asked God, "Why? Why did You have to take Jasmine?"

There will be times when our prayers are not answered the way we want or the way we feel they should be, especially when we pray for God to save our loved ones and it does not happen.

We realized that God was still in the midst of our storm. He kept us from losing our minds and allowed us to continue to stay strong and witness to other families who may have gone through the same type of situation. Circumstances will only make us stronger. That's why it is important that we remain steadfast, rooted, grounded, and always abiding in His Word so that we can continue to build His kingdom one by one, and reach each saint one at a time.

"Therefore, my dear brothers and sisters, stand firm. Let nothing move you. Always give yourselves fully to the work of the Lord, because you know that your labor in the Lord is not in vain"
1 Corinthians 15:58 (NIV).

Who is Jasmine?

Jasmine Macie Elmore was born to Jackie Elmore, Sr. and Adella Elmore of Orangeburg, SC. She left behind two brothers: Jackie Elmore, Jr., and William Elmore. You may wonder why she was so special or different from anyone else. Well, that's the answer…she was different.

When Jasmine was a baby, I would babysit for my sister and brother-in-law. I remember when my daughter, Diamond was just a month old, and Jasmine was four months old. We were at my mother's house, and I watched Diamond and Jasmine as we prepared for a family event. Diamond sat in her carrier, screaming at the top of her lungs. As I tried to quiet her, Jasmine sat up in her carrier and looked over at her as if to say, "Girl, why are you screaming?" This was the attitude Jasmine carried into childhood and young adulthood. I don't remember her crying much about anything. She had a very nonchalant and carefree attitude. She did not hold grudges. If she was mad about something, you were going to know right then and there, and that was the end of it. Every time she saw you, she always greeted you with her arms literally wide open for a big hug. She loved on you even if you didn't want to be loved on.

Jasmine loved both of her parents dearly. She was a Daddy's girl and a Mama's girl. She and her brothers were typical siblings. They had their spats, but if anyone messed with one, you messed with all. Jasmine was raised to love the Lord and respect all those around her. She set an example as to how we should live our lives daily.

I remember a time when a girl did not move over on the sidewalk for my youngest daughter, Emerald. Jasmine thought Emerald belonged to her, so she protected her at all times. She stopped and asked me, "Did you see that?"

I had to calm her down and let her know that it was okay. She did not like seeing others bullied or mistreated, and certainly not her family members. Jasmine stood up for what she believed in, and she stood up for others as well.

"Bear with one another and, if one has a complaint against another, forgive each

*other; just as the Lord has forgiven you,
so you also must forgive"*
Colossians 3:13 (NRS).

Physical Appearance

Jasmine began braiding and styling hair at a very young age. When her father discovered her love for doing hair, he found cosmetology dolls so she could practice.

Not too long ago, Jasmine told me she thought I was a cosmetologist. When I asked her what made her think that, she said, "You always did our hair when we were younger." (Jasmine's mother missed the craft of hair braiding, therefore, I picked up on the skill.)

My sister told us the story of when she did Jasmine's hair for picture day. She went to school with ponytails in her hair and came back home with ponytails. However, when the pictures returned and my sister looked at them, she noticed that Jasmine's hair was straight. Jasmine loosed her hair out for the pictures and plaited it back before returning home.

She developed a unique sense of style at a very young age. Her love for hair and fashion followed her throughout her high school and college years. She was always clean and matching. She knew what she liked and what she wanted.

"It was granted her to clothe herself with fine linen, bright and pure–for the fine linen is the righteous deeds of the saints."
Revelation 19:8 (ESV).

Salvation

Jasmine became saved at a young age. She received a double portion because both her father's family and her mother's family believe in God.

She faithfully attended her home church, Cornerstone Community Church in Orangeburg, SC. One year she attended a mission trip in Greenville, SC, where they painted old houses. She loved attending church and youth events; and she made friends easily.

During the summer, she attended Vacation Bible School at her Aunt Poopie's church. She helped feed the children snacks and whatever her aunt asked her to do.

There were times when Jasmine would leave straight from there to come help me at my church with the Praise Dance Ministry. She was never tired, but always willing to help, even when we traveled to different churches and events to praise dance.

Jasmine's love for the Lord and others was obvious. Her lifestyle influenced many young children to live for the Lord. If I had to think of a scripture to describe her, it would be **James 1:19:** (NIV) *"My dear brothers and sisters, take note of this: Everyone should be quick to listen, slow to speak and slow to become angry."*

Family is everything!

When we lose our loved ones, we should be able to rejoice in the fact that they have gone on to see Jesus. There may be hurt and pain, but we should not walk around holding grudges, being angry at the situation. Let it go! God, nor our loved ones, want us to stop living.

There is no reason to be alone in your situation. The people in your family will help you get through your time of sorrow. You may not feel like spending time with them or your friends or even being a listening ear, but there is actually healing in spending time with others. You get to know them in ways you haven't before. You will find that they may have issues or problems they've been struggling with as well.

If you are a living, breathing being, you have some type of issue. Even the richest person in the world has some type of problem. If you hear someone saying they don't have any problems, please don't believe them. If they have all the money in the world and no one to share it with, that's a problem.

> *"Be kind and compassionate to one another, forgiving each other, just as in Christ God forgave you"*
> **Ephesians 4:32** (NIV).

Jasmine's life was not finished, but it was full.

There were many things Jasmine had left to accomplish. She attended college to become a music teacher. She worked with children during her practicum at Winthrop University. She did a lot and touched the lives of many; however, she was not finished. We will never finish all that God has set for us on this earth.

Through her death and after her death, she continues to touch the lives of her friends and loved ones. We continue to laugh at the good times and cry through the bad. She will forever remain in our hearts.

"You make known to me the path of life; in your presence there is fullness of

joy; at your right hand are pleasures forevermore"
Psalm 16:11 (ESV).

The blessing is in the press. Allow God to use you.

Everyone was saying, "It will get better," but things only seemed to be getting worse. I tried to take my mind off things, but it barely worked. My mood swung up and down and side to side.

People can't possibly know the pain and agony of losing someone so close unless they have experienced it themselves. The pain I feel is as if I birthed my niece myself, so I can't imagine the pain my sister feels inside. I told her if I feel this way, she has to feel a million times worse. I know she fights the grief, but it can't be easy. For me, some days are worse than others.

Three days after Jasmine's burial, I debated whether I would attend a writing workshop that started at 9:00 a.m. Jasmine's godmother and I got there close to 11:30 a.m. I thought I was going for one thing but ended up going for another. I went looking for information on publishing books, but instead ended up sharing my story. My publisher asked me to talk about my first book. I could not help but share information from my experience that week. Afterwards, several people said they were going to purchase my book and wanted contact information. Book sales and speaking engagements were the last things on my mind, but God continued to speak to me, saying, "There are too many people out there who need your help." The Lord, in His infinite wisdom, made me realize that my testimony will help others through their loss.

It is during these times; we must remember **Philippians 4:13**: *"I can do all thing through Christ who strengthens me"* (NKJV).

The Healing Process

Healing takes time. The process differs from one person to the next. There are steps you can take that will help you move forward. I have learned that a person must do things differently. Try something you've never tried before. Do something you've always wanted to do like horseback riding, getting a massage, or flying on an airplane. Look for promotions or Groupons. You can have fun without spending a lot of money.

Create memories and share them with your children. There's nothing worse than trying to get your children and grandchildren to remember a person, place, or event. Taking pictures and being able to show them these memories helps build them up.

I have learned that it is okay to cry, scream, holler, kick, or do whatever I need to do to get it out. Others may not understand, but it is okay. It is not for them to understand. You may hear people say, "Oh, they are crying because they did not do what they were supposed to, and they feel a sense of guilt."

That is a lie from the pits of hell! If someone hits you in the head with a brick, you will certainly yell. Why is it any different if you feel the emotional pain from the death of a loved one? Give yourself permission to do what you need to do to work toward your healing.

There will be days in which you just don't feel like doing anything. Your body may feel like it just won't move. You may feel tired, beat, or worn. Know that the body is designed to heal itself and gives us signals for what it needs. If you are tired, get some rest.

I had mornings where I couldn't seem to get out of bed and all I could do was lay there until the storm passed. I wasn't sure what triggered it, but I just felt depressed and didn't want to be around people. When depression creeps in, we must remind ourselves that there are others who have been through the same or similar situations. It's okay to allow yourself to have a moment every now and then. However, if it becomes more regular, maybe you should see a doctor.

"Weeping may endure for a night, but joy cometh in the morning"
Psalm 30:5b (KJV)

Afterword

When Jasmine passed, it was a painful feeling as though my child was snatched right out of my hands. It was a feeling of numbness. I could not physically, emotionally, or mentally feel anything at all. I not only cried physically but knew what it was like to feel my spirit cry. Thank God my mind allowed me to think and call on Him. He was the Person who had given me the inner comfort and peace I needed when I did not know what else to do. It was only by God's grace and mercy that I was able to maintain my sanity. To watch my child that I loved so dearly, here one day and gone the next, was the most devastating thing I have ever experienced in my life. But this was also one of the times that I felt God's presence more than ever. God, who says in His word, "*I will never leave you nor forsake you,"* was there with me (**Hebrews 13:5**, ESV).

With good intentions, people often say, "Sorry for your loss." But, I don't see it as a loss. It is a separation that often comes unseen too soon.

While traveling through a small town I often drive through, in my moment of grieving, the Lord diverted my attention to notice things I had not paid attention to in the past. I took mental notes and realized how different the town looked. The Holy Spirit spoke to me and said, "Everything has a time, but God is the clock keeper."

As I conversed back and forth with God, I understood that to mean everyone has a set time to be on earth, but God with His glorious power can shorten or extend our time here. He brought to my memory, as it is written in His Word, "*And I hold the keys of death and Hades*" (**Revelation 1:18**, NIV).

It is puzzling how sometimes things we do not imagine in life seem to happen and the things we do imagine sometimes never seem to take place.

I found myself standing over my daughter's casket thanking and praising God, but later wondering why I was able to do that at that time. Then I remembered the scripture **1 Thessalonians 5:18:** "*In everything give thanks*" (NKJV). That is not only in good things that are pleasing to us, but in everything. Then I heard a whisper in my spirit say, "Give thanks because I am God! God Almighty!"

People have said to me, and I can sometimes see it on their faces, "How can you go on after the death of your daughter?"

It is not only with knowing that God is present in my life, but that He has given me strength to endure. I remember God's Word spoken so clearly in my ears between the time of Jasmine's passing and the funeral. He said to me, "Tomorrow is not promised, and we don't know the hour I will come or call." Certainly, I could not be angry with God because this has already been said in His Word.

Jasmine was very precious to my husband and me. Nothing could ever take the place she holds in our hearts. I will always remember and cherish her smile and our momma-daughter talks and the phone calls when she would address me, "Hey, lady" and ask, "Where's that man?" (referring to her father)

The devil came against my family and me in the worst way. Death attacked my daughter, but God gets the glory. Because we are made of flesh and bones, we will experience physical and emotional pain, but God has the final say in all things.

After the announcing of her passing, God, the clock keeper, quietly spoke to me, "Her spirit has gone on. Her assignment here on earth has ended."

I told God, "I wish my daughter could come home as she did on weekends from college.
The Lord spoke and said, "She is home."
Adella Elmore

In Loving Memory

Jasmine Macie Elmore

Gone, but not forgotten!

January 26, 1998 – May 9, 2018

About the Author

LaVetra Sullivan lives in Orangeburg, South Carolina. She has two wonderful daughters, Diamond and Emerald, from a fourteen-year marriage.

She is a 1991 graduate of Kingstree Senior High School in Kingstree, SC. In 1995, she obtained a Bachelor of Arts degree in English with a minor in Mass Communications from Francis Marion University in Florence, SC. In 2005, she earned a Master's degree of Education in Literacy: Curriculum and

Instruction from Lesley University in Cambridge, Massachusetts.

In 2003, LaVetra began teaching at Calhoun County High School in St. Matthews, SC. She has taught ninth through twelfth grade English for the past twenty years. In addition, she has taught Reading, Journalism, African American Literature, Public Speaking, and Drama. She currently serves as English Department Chairperson. LaVetra has also served as Teacher of the Year, Freshman Academy Lead Teacher, After School Homework Center Coordinator, and advisor for various clubs and organizations.

Her goals include continuing her studies and making an impact on society through writing. In 2017, LaVetra published her first book, *Can I Borrow Some Trust?*

Her favorite scripture is **Jeremiah 29:11**: (NIV) *"For I know the plans I have for you," declares the Lord, "plans to prosper you and not to harm you, plans to give you hope and a future."*

www.ingramcontent.com/pod-product-compliance
Lightning Source LLC
Chambersburg PA
CBHW041508010526
44118CB00006B/190